Mums Are Like Buttons

They hold everything together

Edited by Emma Marriott

MACMILLAN

First published 2015 by Macmillan
an imprint of Pan Macmillan, a division of Macmillan Publishers Limited
Pan Macmillan, 20 New Wharf Road, London N1 9RR
Basingstoke and Oxford
Associated companies throughout the world
www.panmacmillan.com

ISBN 978-1-4472-9284-5

9 8 7 6 5 4 3 2 1

A CIP catalogue record for this book is available from the British Library.

Designed by Perfect Bound Ltd

Printed and bound by Printer Trento S.r.l.

Visit www.panmacmillan.com to read more about all our books and to buy them.
You will also find features, author interviews and news of any author events, and you
can sign up for e-newsletters so that you're always first to hear about our new releases.

TO

. . . .

WITH LOVE FROM

. . . .

Being
a mother
is learning about
strengths you didn't
know you had, and
dealing with fears
you didn't know
existed.

LINDA WOOTEN

God
could not be
everywhere,
so He created
mothers.

JEWISH PROVERB

FOR THE HAND THAT ROCKS THE CRADLE

IS THE HAND THAT RULES THE WORLD.

WILLIAM ROSS WALLACE

8

All women become
like their mothers.
That is their tragedy.

No man does.
That's his.

OSCAR WILDE

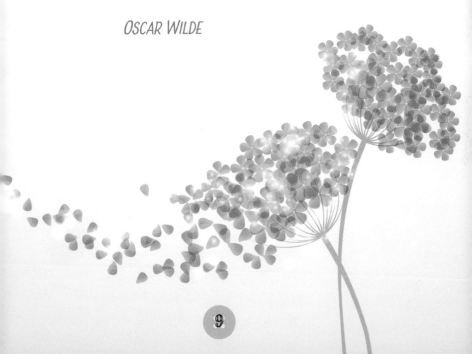

Call your mother.
Tell her you love her.
Remember, you're the only person who knows
what her heart sounds like from the inside.

RACHEL WOLCHIN

And Polly didn't think she had done much; but it was one of the little things which are always waiting to be done in this world of ours, where rainy days come so often, where spirits get out of tune, and duty won't go hand in hand with pleasure. Little things of this sort are especially good work for little people; a kind little thought, an unselfish little act, a cheery little word, are so sweet and comfortable, that no one can fail to feel their beauty and love the giver, no matter how small they are. Mothers do a deal of this sort of thing, unseen, unthanked, but felt and remembered long afterward, and never lost, for this is the simple magic that binds hearts together, and keeps home happy.

LOUISA MAY ALCOTT

There's nothing like your mother's sympathetic voice to make you want to burst into tears.

SOPHIE KINSELLA

She was a
MONSTER,
but she was
MY monster.

JEANETTE WINTERSON

*A mother's love for her child
is like nothing else in the world.
It knows no law, no pity.
It dares all things and
crushes down remorselessly
all that stands in its path.*

AGATHA CHRISTIE

What DO girls do who haven't any mothers to help them through their troubles?

LOUISA MAY ALCOTT

My mother . . . she is beautiful,
softened at the edges
and tempered with a spine
of steel. I want to grow
old and be like her.

JODI PICOULT

Life began with waking up and loving my mother's face.

GEORGE ELIOT

LOVE IS A
ROLLER COASTER.
MOTHERHOOD
IS A WHOLE
AMUSEMENT
PARK.

CATHY GUISEWITE

A woman has two smiles
that an angel might envy –
the smile that accepts a lover before
words are uttered, and the smile
that lights on the first-born babe,
and assures it of a mother's love.

THOMAS C. HALIBURTON

MY MOTHER HAD A GOOD DEAL OF TROUBLE WITH ME, BUT I THINK SHE ENJOYED IT.

MARK TWAIN

A mother's heart is a patchwork of love.

ANONYMOUS

23

GUILT IS TO MOTHERHOOD AS GRAPES ARE TO WINE.

FAY WELDON

Mother
is a verb,
not a noun.

PROVERB

Youth fades; love droops,
    the leaves of friendship fall;
a mother's secret hope outlives them all.

OLIVER WENDELL HOLMES

ALL
MOTHERS
ARE
WORKING
MOTHERS.

ANONYMOUS

Nobody can have the soul of me.
My mother has had it, and nobody can
have it again. Nobody can come into my self
again, and breathe me like an atmosphere.

D. H. LAWRENCE

Children are
the anchors that
hold a mother
to life.

SOPHOCLES

Hundreds of dewdrops to greet the dawn,
Hundreds of bees in the purple clover,
Hundreds of butterflies on the lawn,
But only one mother the wide world over.

GEORGE COOPER

30

31

A man loves his
sweetheart the most,
his wife the best,
but his mother
the longest.

IRISH PROVERB

The angels, whispering to one another,
Can find, among their burning terms of love,
None so devotional as that of 'Mother'.

EDGAR ALLAN POE

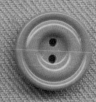

A mother, a real mother with a little child, thinks day and night about the welfare of the little one in her arms. A mother knows what dangers the child will have to encounter as he grows up. She does not let the father reassure her when he makes light of things and says that the children have to find their own way.

A mother worries, for she carries the burden, and she often sees much deeper than the father just where the child is in danger.

JOHANN CHRISTOPH BLUMHARDT

35

All that I am
my mother
made me.

JOHN QUINCY ADAMS

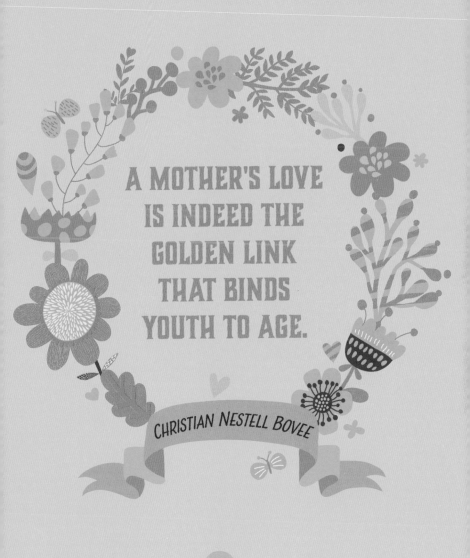

A MOTHER'S LOVE
IS INDEED THE
GOLDEN LINK
THAT BINDS
YOUTH TO AGE.

CHRISTIAN NESTELL BOVEE

37

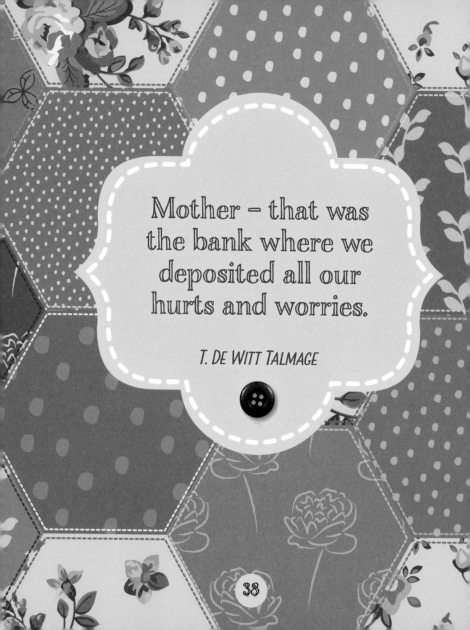

Mother – that was the bank where we deposited all our hurts and worries.

T. DE WITT TALMAGE

38

I believe that always, or almost always, in all childhoods and in all the lives that follow them, the mother represents madness. Our mothers always remain the strangest, craziest people we've ever met.

MARGUERITE DURAS

A mother is the truest friend we have, when trials, heavy and sudden, fall upon us: when adversity takes the place of prosperity; when friends who rejoice with us in our sunshine, desert us when troubles thicken around us, still will she cling to us, and endeavour by her kind precepts and counsels to dissipate the clouds of darkness, and cause peace to return to our hearts.

WASHINGTON IRVING

LET FRANCE HAVE GOOD MOTHERS AND SHE WILL HAVE GOOD SONS.

NAPOLEON BONAPARTE

It is the nightly custom of every good mother after her children are asleep to rummage in their minds and put things straight for next morning, repacking into their proper places the many articles that have wandered during the day. If you could keep awake (but of course you can't) you would see your own mother doing this, and you would find it very interesting to watch her. It is quite like tidying up drawers. You would see her on her knees, I expect, lingering humorously over

some of your contents, wondering
where on earth you had picked this
thing up, making discoveries sweet
and not so sweet, pressing this to her
cheek as if it were as nice as a kitten,
and hurriedly stowing that out of sight.
When you wake in the morning, the
naughtinesses and evil passions with
which you went to bed have been folded
up small and placed at the bottom of
your mind; and on the top, beautifully
aired, are spread out prettier thoughts,
ready for you to put on.

J. M. BARRIE

Heaven is at the feet of mothers.

PERSIAN PROVERB

A man's mother is so tissued and woven into his life and brain that he can no more describe her than describe the air and sunlight that bless his days.

To walk and talk with them is like slipping on an old coat. To hear their voices is like the shake of music in a sober evening hush.

CHRISTOPHER MORLEY

O Mrs Higden, Mrs Higden,
you was a woman and
a mother, and a mangler
in a million million.

CHARLES DICKENS

My mother had a slender, small body, but a large heart – a heart so large that everybody's joys found welcome in it, and hospitable accommodation.

MARK TWAIN

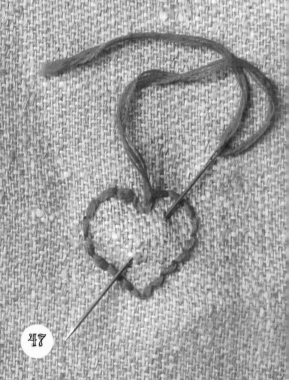

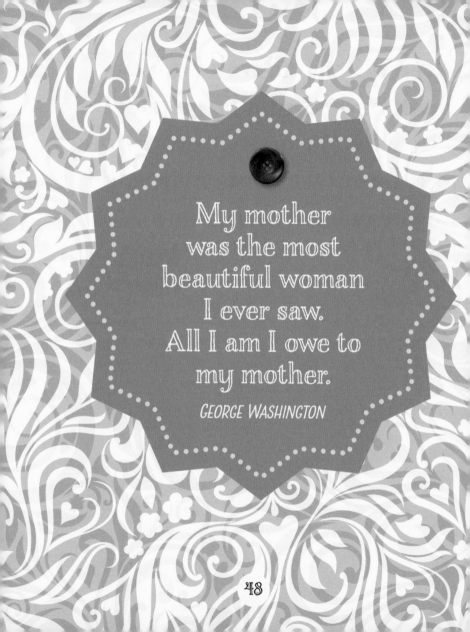

My mother
was the most
beautiful woman
I ever saw.
All I am I owe to
my mother.

GEORGE WASHINGTON

Making the decision to
have a child -- it's momentous.
It is to decide forever to have
your heart go walking around
outside your body.

Elizabeth Stone

49

I love my mother as the trees love water and sunshine – she helps me grow, prosper, and reach great heights.

ADABELLA RADICI

Bold, quick,
ingenious,
forward, capable;
He's all the
mother's, from
the top to toe.

WILLIAM SHAKESPEARE

A mother is she who can take the place of all others, but whose place no one else can take.

CARDINAL MERMILLOD

The greatest love
is a mother's,
then a dog's,
then a
sweetheart's.

POLISH PROVERB

No language can express the power, and beauty, and heroism, and majesty of a mother's love. It shrinks not where man cowers, and grows stronger where man faints, and over wastes of worldly fortunes sends the radiance of its quenchless fidelity like a star.

EDWIN HUBBELL CHAPIN

The heart of a mother is a deep abyss
at the bottom of which you will always
find forgiveness.

HONORÉ DE BALZAC

NO ONE IN THE WORLD CAN TAKE THE PLACE OF YOUR MOTHER.

HARRY S. TRUMAN

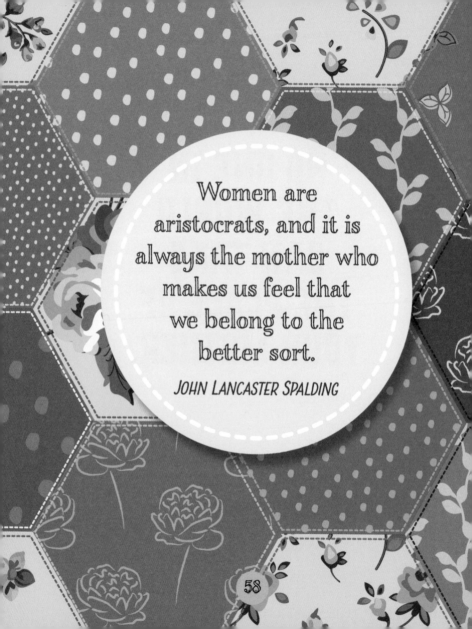

Women are
aristocrats, and it is
always the mother who
makes us feel that
we belong to the
better sort.

JOHN LANCASTER SPALDING

THERE IS ONLY ONE PRETTY CHILD IN THE WORLD, AND EVERY MOTHER HAS IT.

CHINESE PROVERB

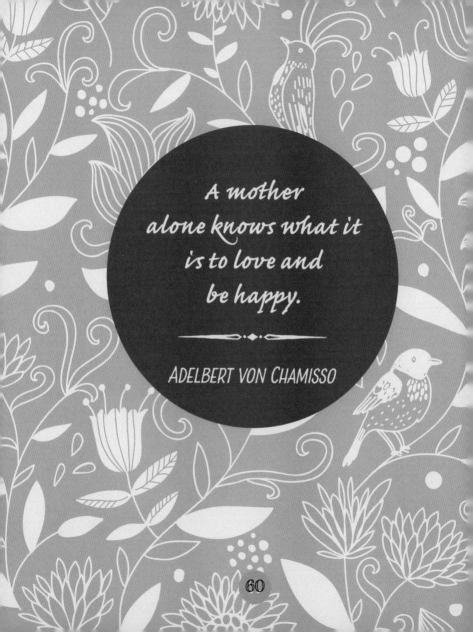

A mother
alone knows what it
is to love and
be happy.

ADELBERT VON CHAMISSO

Mother-love is the fuel that enables a normal human being to do the impossible.

MARION C. GARRETTY

Mother's arms are
made of tenderness,
And sweet sleep
blesses the child
who lies therein.

VICTOR HUGO

A MUM'S HUG LASTS
LONG AFTER SHE LETS GO.

ANONYMOUS

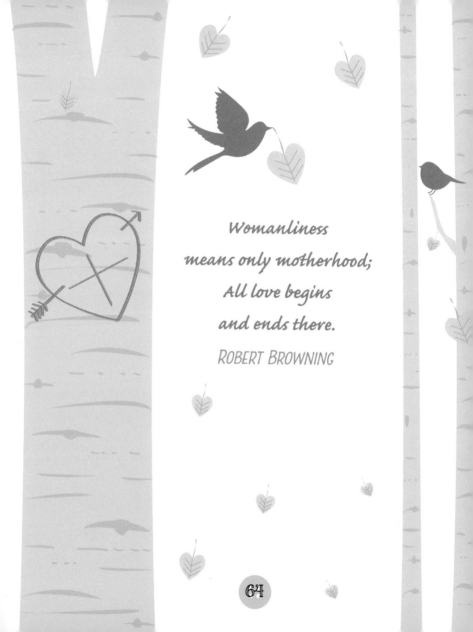

Womanliness
means only motherhood;
All love begins
and ends there.

ROBERT BROWNING

A mother is not
to be compared with
another person.
She is incomparable.

AFRICAN PROVERB

MOTHER, THE RIBBONS OF YOUR LOVE ARE WOVEN AROUND MY HEART.

ANONYMOUS

Every beetle is a gazelle
in the eye of its mother.

MOORISH PROVERB

67

She was of the stuff
of which great men's mothers
are made. She was indispensable
to high generation, hated at tea
parties, feared in shops,
and loved at crises.

THOMAS HARDY

Here's to the happiest
days of my life,
Spent in the arms of
another man's wife –
My mother's.

TRADITIONAL TOAST

The clocks were striking midnight and the rooms were very still as a figure glided quietly from bed to bed, smoothing a coverlet here, settling a pillow there, and pausing to look long and tenderly at each unconscious face, to kiss each with lips that mutely blessed, and to pray the fervent prayers which only mothers utter.

LOUISA MAY ALCOTT

A mother understands
what a child does not say.

JEWISH PROVERB

Mama exhorted her children at every opportunity to 'jump at de sun'. We might not land on the sun, but at least we would get off the ground.

Zora Neale Hurston

Motherhood is a choice you make every day, to put someone else's happiness and well-being ahead of your own, to teach the hard lessons, to do the right thing even when you're not sure what the right thing is . . . and to forgive yourself, over and over again, for doing everything wrong.

DONNA BALL

The mother memories that are closest to my heart are the small gentle ones that I have carried over from the days of my childhood. They are not profound, but they have stayed with me through life, and when I am very old, they will still be near . . .

Memories of mother drying
my tears, reading aloud, cutting
cookies and singing as she did,
listening to prayers I said as I
knelt with my forehead pressed
against her knee, tucking me in
bed and turning down the light.
They have carried me through
the years and given my life such
a firm foundation that it does not
rock beneath flood or tempest.

MARGARET SANGSTER

Poor Dan clung to her in speechless gratitude, feeling the blessedness of mother love – that divine gift which comforts, purifies, and strengthens all who seek it.

LOUISA MAY ALCOTT

M others were much too sharp. They were like dogs. Buster always sensed when anything was out of the ordinary, and so did mothers. Mothers and dogs both had a kind of second sight that made them see into people's minds and know when anything unusual was going on.

ENID BLYTON

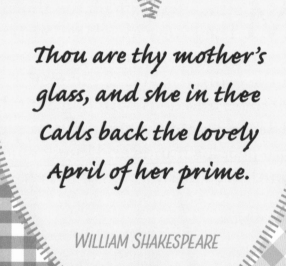

Thou are thy mother's glass, and she in thee Calls back the lovely April of her prime.

WILLIAM SHAKESPEARE

Who ran to help me when I fell,
And would some pretty story tell,
Or kiss the place to make it well?
My Mother.

ANN TAYLOR AND JANE TAYLOR

It's a funny thing about mothers and fathers. Even when their own child is the most **DISGUSTING LITTLE BLISTER** you could ever imagine, they still think that he or she is **WONDERFUL.**

ROALD DAHL

How many hopes and fears,
how many ardent wishes
and anxious apprehensions,
are twisted together in the
threads that connect the
parent with the child!

SAMUEL G. GOODRICH

MOTHERS HOLD THEIR CHILDREN'S HANDS FOR A MOMENT, BUT THEIR HEARTS FOR EVER.

ANONYMOUS

Mother! What a world of affection is comprised in that single word; how little do we in the giddy round of youthful pleasure and folly heed her wise counsels. How lightly do we look upon that zealous care with which she guides our otherwise erring feet, and watches with feelings which none but a mother can know the gradual expansion of our youth to the riper years of discretion. We may not think of it then, but it will be recalled to our minds in after years, when the gloomy grave or a fearful living separation has placed

her far beyond our reach, and her sweet voice of sympathy and consolation for the various ills attendant upon us sounds in our ears no more. How deeply then we regret a thousand deeds that we have done contrary to her gentle admonitions! How we sigh for those days once more, that we may retrieve what we have done amiss and make her kind heart glad with happiness! Alas! Once gone they can never be recalled, and we grow mournfully sad with the bitter reflection.

FANNY KELLY

Maybe we're all like that with our mothers. They seem ordinary until one day they're extraordinary.

LISA SEE

Mother did not spend all her time in paying dull calls to dull ladies, and sitting dully at home waiting for dull ladies to pay calls to her. She was almost always there, ready to play with the children, and read to them, and help them to do their home-lessons. Besides this she used to write stories for them while they were at school, and read them aloud after tea, and she always made up funny pieces of poetry for their birthdays and for other great occasions, such as the christening of the new kittens, or the refurnishing of the doll's house, or the time when they were getting over the mumps.

E. NESBIT

89

Blest the Babe,

Nursed in his Mother's arms, who sinks to sleep

Rocked on his Mother's breast; who with his soul

Drinks in the feelings of his Mother's eye!

For him, in one dear Presence, there exists

A virtue which irradiates and exalts

Objects through widest intercourse of sense.

WILLIAM WORDSWORTH

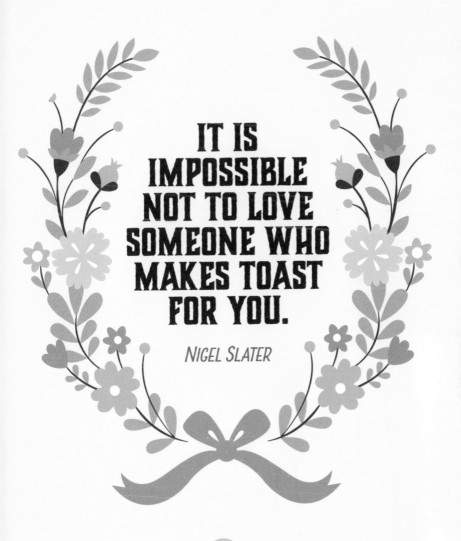

IT IS
IMPOSSIBLE
NOT TO LOVE
SOMEONE WHO
MAKES TOAST
FOR YOU.

NIGEL SLATER

ONE GOOD MOTHER IS WORTH A HUNDRED SCHOOLMASTERS.

PROVERB

92

My mother, freed from her noisy day, would sleep like a happy child, humped in her nightdress, breathing innocently and making soft drinking sounds in the pillow. In her flights of dream she held me close, like a parachute to her back; or rolled and enclosed me with her great tired body so that I was snug as a mouse in a hayrick.

LAURIE LEE

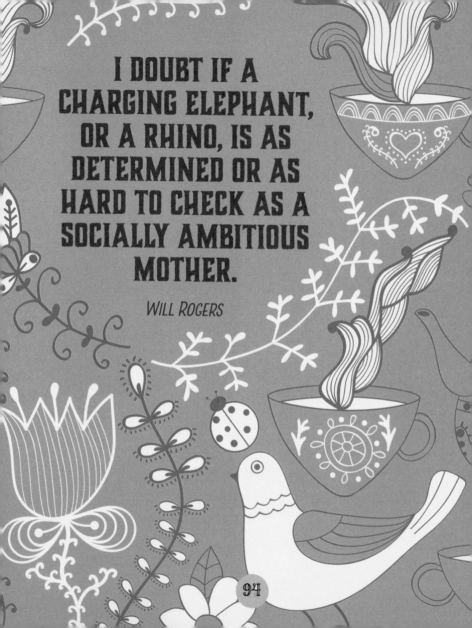

I DOUBT IF A CHARGING ELEPHANT, OR A RHINO, IS AS DETERMINED OR AS HARD TO CHECK AS A SOCIALLY AMBITIOUS MOTHER.

WILL ROGERS

94

Mother, dear mother, the years have been long

Since I last listened your lullaby song:

Sing, then, and unto my soul it shall seem

Womanhood's years have been only a dream.

ELIZABETH CHASE AKERS ALLEN

There is a reason people say being a mother is the hardest job in the world: you do not sleep and you do not get vacation time. You do not leave your work on your desk at the end of the day. Your briefcase is your heart, and you are rifling through it constantly. Your office is as wide as the world, and your punch card is measured not in hours but in a lifetime.

JODI PICOULT

96

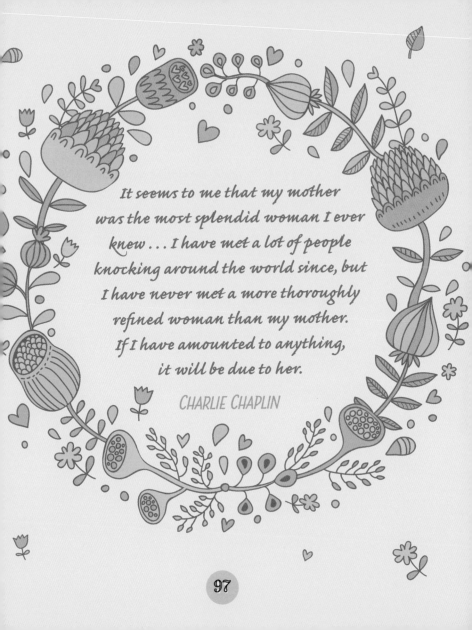

It seems to me that my mother
was the most splendid woman I ever
knew ... I have met a lot of people
knocking around the world since, but
I have never met a more thoroughly
refined woman than my mother.
If I have amounted to anything,
it will be due to her.

CHARLIE CHAPLIN

Sonnets are full of love, and this my tome

Has many sonnets: so here now shall be

One sonnet more, a love sonnet, from me

To her whose heart is my heart's quiet home,

To my first Love, my Mother, on whose knee

I learnt love-lore that is not troublesome;

Whose service is my special dignity,

And she my loadstar while I go and come
And so because you love me, and because
I love you, Mother, I have woven a wreath
Of rhymes wherewith to crown your honoured name:
In you not fourscore years can dim the flame
Of love, whose blessed glow transcends the laws
Of time and change and mortal life and death.

CHRISTINA ROSSETTI

Women know
The way to rear up children (to be just)
They know a simple, merry, tender knack
Of tying sashes, fitting baby shoes,
And stringing pretty words that make no sense,
And kissing full sense into empty words.

ELIZABETH BARRETT BROWNING

When you die, your sister's tears
will dry as time goes on,
your widow's tears will
cease in another's arms,
but your mother will mourn
you till the day she dies.

ARAB PROVERB

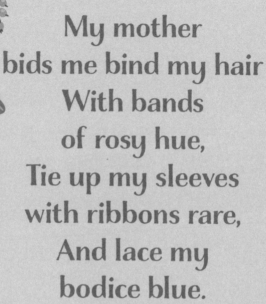

My mother
bids me bind my hair
With bands
of rosy hue,
Tie up my sleeves
with ribbons rare,
And lace my
bodice blue.

ANNE HUNTER

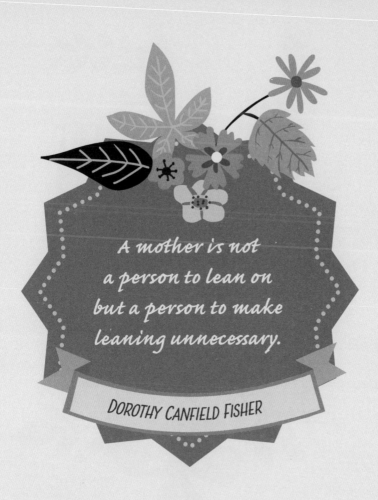

A mother is not
a person to lean on
but a person to make
leaning unnecessary.

DOROTHY CANFIELD FISHER

MEN ARE WHAT THEIR MOTHERS MADE THEM.

RALPH WALDO EMERSON

*I have reached the age
when a woman begins to perceive
that she is growing into the person
she least plans to resemble: her mother.*

ANITA BROOKNER

The mother's yearning, that completest
type of the life in another life
which is the essence of real human love,
feels the presence of the cherished child
even in the debased, degraded man.

GEORGE ELIOT

If I were damned of body and soul,
I know whose prayers
would make me whole,
Mother o' mine, O mother o' mine.

RUDYARD KIPLING

Mothers are the only race of people that speak the same tongue. A mother in Manchuria could converse with a mother in Nebraska and never miss a word.

WILL ROGERS

He that would
the daughter win
Must with the mother
first begin.

JOHN RAY

LIKE MOTHER, LIKE DAUGHTER.

SIXTEENTH-CENTURY PROVERB

Mighty is the force of motherhood! It transforms all things by its vital heat; it turns timidity into fierce courage, and dreadless defiance into tremulous submission; it turns thoughtlessness into foresight, and yet stills all anxiety into calm content; it makes selfishness become self-denial, and gives even to hard vanity the glance of admiring love.

GEORGE ELIOT

A mother is always the beginning. She is how things begin.

AMY TAN

Father, Mother, and Me,
Sister and Auntie say
All the people like us are We,
And everyone else is They.

RUDYARD KIPLING

Most of all the other beautiful things in life come by twos and threes, by dozens and hundreds. Plenty of roses, stars, sunsets, rainbows, brothers and sisters, aunts and cousins, but only one mother in the whole world.

KATE DOUGLAS WIGGIN

They say there is no other
Can take the place of mother.

GEORGE BERNARD SHAW

The world has no such flowers in any land,

And no such pearl in any gulf the sea,

As any babe on any mother's knee.

ALGERNON CHARLES SWINBURNE

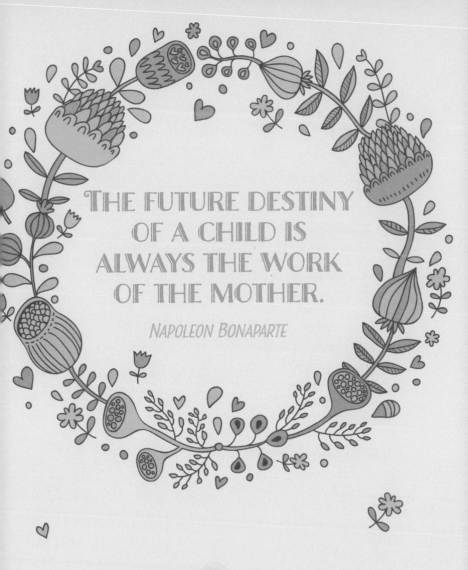

THE FUTURE DESTINY
OF A CHILD IS
ALWAYS THE WORK
OF THE MOTHER.

Napoleon Bonaparte

Children, look into those eyes,
listen to the dear voice, notice
the feeling of even a single touch
that is bestowed upon you by that
gentle hand! Make much of it while
yet you have that most precious
of all good gifts – a loving mother.
Read the unfathomable love of those
eyes, the kind anxiety of that tone
and look, however slight your pain.
In afterlife you may have friends,
and dear friends, but never will you
have again the inexpressible love
and gentleness lavished upon you,
which none but mother bestows.

THOMAS BABINGTON MACAULAY

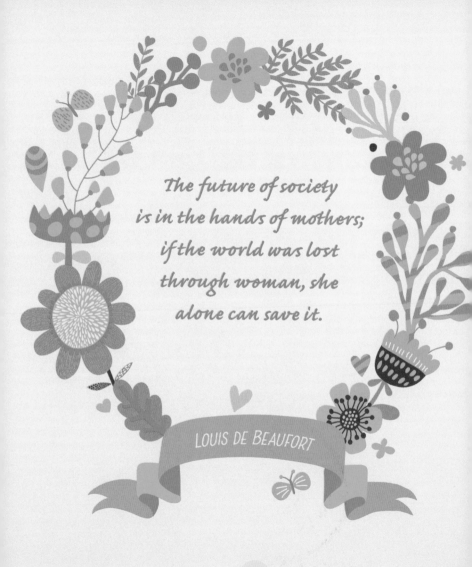

The future of society
is in the hands of mothers;
if the world was lost
through woman, she
alone can save it.

LOUIS DE BEAUFORT

My mother loved
children – she would
have given anything
if I'd been one.

Groucho Marx

123

Where there is
a mother in the house,
matters speed well.

A. B. ALCOTT

Nature's
loving proxy,
the watchful
mother.

EDWARD GEORGE BULWER-LYTTON

125

Is not a young mother
one of the sweetest sights
which life shows us?

WILLIAM MAKEPEACE THACKERAY

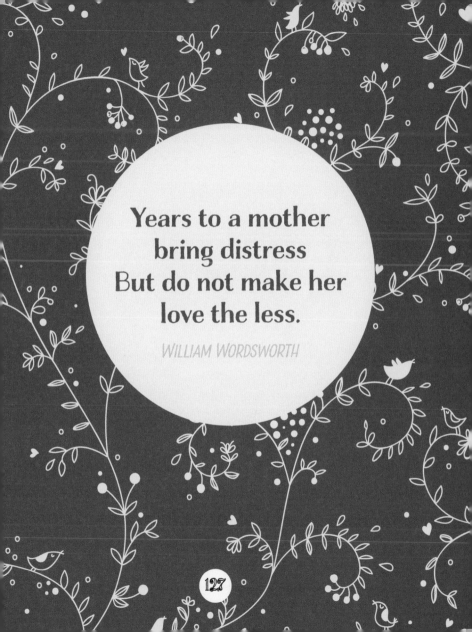

Years to a mother
bring distress
But do not make her
love the less.

WILLIAM WORDSWORTH

He that wipes
the child's nose
kisseth the
mother's cheek.

GEORGE HERBERT

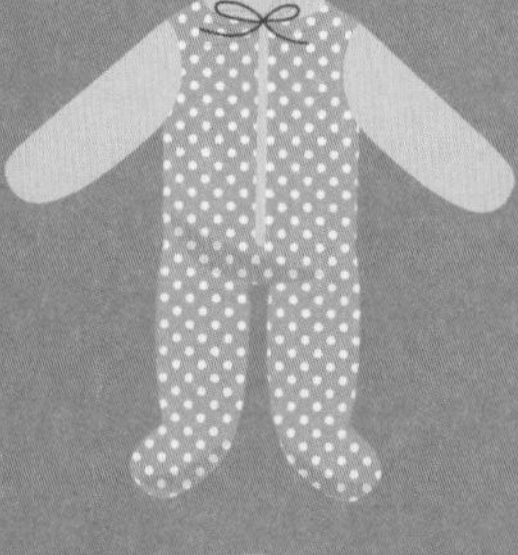

Thou, while thy babes around thee cling,
Shalt show us how divine a thing
A woman may be made.

WILLIAM WORDSWORTH

The mother's heart
is the child's schoolroom.

HENRY WARD BEECHER

The mother's love is at first
an absorbing delight,
blunting all other sensibilities;
it is an expansion of the animal existence.

GEORGE ELIOT

You taught me
to listen to how I feel
and always have a back-up plan.

ANONYMOUS

The tie which links mother and child is of such pure and immaculate strength as to be never violated, except by those whose feelings are withered by vitiated society. Holy, simple, and beautiful in its construction, it is the emblem of all we can imagine of fidelity and truth.

WASHINGTON IRVING

NOT ALWAYS EYE TO EYE

BUT ALWAYS HEART TO HEART.

ANONYMOUS

There is nothing more charming
than to see a mother with a child in her arms,
and nothing more venerable
than a mother among a number of her children.

JOHANN WOLFGANG VON GOETHE

VIRTUE
AND
HAPPINESS
ARE
MOTHER
AND
DAUGHTER.

H. G. BOHN

'Can anything harm us, Mother,
after the night-lights are lit?'
'Nothing, precious,' she said,
'they are the eyes a mother leaves
behind her to guard her children.'
She went from bed to bed singing
enchantments over them, and little
Michael flung his arms round her.
'Mother,' he cried, 'I'm glad of you.'

J. M. BARRIE

Sooner or later
we all quote
our mothers.

BERNARD WILLIAMS

What is home without a mother?

ALICE HAWTHORNE

Acknowledgements

Works in copyright

Donna Ball from *At Home on Ladybug Farm* © 2009 by Donna Ball. Used by permission of The Berkley Publishing Group, a division of Penguin Group (USA) LLC; Enid Blyton from *The Mystery of the Hidden House*, permission granted by Hodder & Stoughton (Enid Blyton Estate), 338 Euston Road, London NW1 3BH; Anita Brookner from *Incidents in the Rue Laugier* © Anita Brookner 1996, reprinted by permission of A. M. Heath & Co Ltd; Charlie Chaplin by permission of Roy Export S.A.S; Agatha Christie from *The Hound of Death* ©1933 Agatha Christie Limited. All rights reserved. Reprinted by permission of HarperCollins Publishers Ltd and Agatha Christie Limited. AGATHA CHRISTIE is a registered trademark of Agatha Christie Limited in the UK and/or elsewhere. All rights reserved; Roald Dahl from *Matilda* © 1988 Roald Dahl. Published in the UK by Jonathan Cape Ltd and Penguin Books Ltd and reprinted by permission of David Higham Associates Limited on behalf of the Roald Dahl Estate and Puffin Books, a division of Penguin Group (USA) LLC; Marguerite Duras from *La Vie Matérielle* © P.O.L Editeur, 1987; Zora Neale Hurston from *Dust Tracks on a Road* ©1942 by Zora Neale Hurston. Renewed © 1970 by John C. Hurston. Reprinted by permission of HarperCollins publishers and Virago Press/Little, Brown Book Group; Sophie Kinsella from *The Secret Dreamworld of a Shopaholic* © Sophie Kinsella 2000, reprinted by permission of Lucas Alexander Whitley; D. H. Lawrence from *The Selected Letters of D. H. Lawrence* © Cambridge University Press 1997, reprinted by permission of Pollinger Limited (www.pollingerltd.com) on behalf of the Estate of Frieda Lawrence Ravagli; Laurie Lee reproduced with permission of Curtis Brown Group Ltd, London on behalf of The Estate of Laurie Lee © Laurie Lee 1959; Christopher Morley by permission of the Christopher Morley Literary Estate;

Jodi Picoult (page 96 from *Larger than Life* © 2014 Jodi Picoult) by permission of Jodi Picoult and the Laura Gross Literary Agency and Hodder & Stoughton Limited; Lisa See from *Shanghai Girls*, reprinted by permission of the Sandra Dijkstra Literary Agency; George Bernard Shaw from *The Admirable Bashville*, reprinted by permission of The Society of Authors, on behalf of the Bernard Shaw Estate; Nigel Slater from *Toast* © Nigel Slater 2003, reprinted by permission of Lucas Alexander Whitley Ltd; Fay Weldon from *She May Not Leave,* used by permission of Capel & Land Ltd; Amy Tan from *The Bonesetter's Daughter*, reprinted by permission of the Sandra Dijkstra Literary Agency; Jeanette Winterson from *Why Be Happy When You Could Be Normal?*, reprinted by permission of Peters Fraser & Dunlop (www.petersfraserdunlop.com) on behalf of Jeanette Winterson. Thanks also to Cathy Guisewite, Rachel Wolchin and Elizabeth Stone for granting the publishers permission to reproduce their work.

Illustrations

Shutterstock.com: Acter page 140; Alla.ya pages 8, 29, 48; AndreKart Photography page 66; April Turner pages 98-9; bernashafo page 59; Click Bestsellers pages 9, 132; Dmitry Zimin page 51; Helen Bloom page 81; Irmairma pages 12, 63; irur pages 72-3; Iveta Angelova page 83; Jenn Huls cover and pages 1, 3, 10, 135; Jordi C page 16; josefauer pages 8, 10, 22-23, 38, 48, 59, 80, 124-125; Ksenia Palimski page 106; LenLis pages 18-19, 26-7, 32, 52-3, 56-7, 59, 61, 78-80, 90-91, 101, 104-5, 129, 144; mama_mia page 77; Markova pages 84, 94-5, 109, 133; monbibi pages 92-3; NuDesign.co pages 38, 58; photocell page 33; PinkPueblo pages 50, 110; Preto Perola pages 124-5; Shemoto pages 24-5; Sinelyov page 47; smilewithjul pages 7, 35, 37, 44-5, 60, 68-9, 74, 84-7, 96-7, 114, 118-9, 121-3, 127, 137-9; Tatiana Kasyanova pages 22-3, 80; tatianat pages 100, 130-1; xenia_ok pages 20, 128.

All other illustrations: Mia Charro.